ANIMAL ATHLETICS

Isabel Thomas

raintree

a Capstone company — publishers for children

Raintree is an imprint of Capstone Global Library Limited, a company incorporated in England and Wales having its registered office at 264 Banbury Road, Oxford OX2 7DY – Registered company number: 6695582

www.raintree.co.uk
myorders@raintree.co.uk

Edited by Linda Staniford
Designed by Steve Mead
Picture research by Kelly Garvin
Production by Victoria Fitzgerald
Originated by Capstone Global Library Ltd
Printed and bound in China

ISBN 978 1 474 71359 7
19 18 17 16 15
10 9 8 7 6 5 4 3 2 1

British Library Cataloguing in Publication Data
A full catalogue record for this book is available from the British Library.

Acknowledgements
We would like to thank the following for permission to reproduce photographs:
Corbis/Stephen Krasemann/All Canada Photos, 16; Getty Images: Al Tielemans/Sports Illustrated, 10, Bill Frakes/Sports Illustrated, 6, Stu Forster, 18; Glow Images/DLILLC/Corbis, 25; iStockphoto/Dirk Freder, 26; Minden Pictures: Atsuo Fujimaru, 13, Konrad Wothe, 8, Satoshi Kuribayashi, cover (top left), Stephen Dalton, 13, 20, ZSSD, 24; Newscom: Davy Adam/PA Photos/ABACA, 4, Gerard Lacz/VWPics, 7, Julian Stratenschulte/dpa/picture-alliance, 27, Kieran Galvin/Actionplus, 22, Mark Blinch/Rueters, 14, Matthias Breiter/Minden Pictures, 12, Michael Durham/Minden Pictures, 19, Wil Meinderts/Buiten-beeld/Minden Pictures, 23; Shutterstock: Cat Downie, 5, kingfisher, 9, paula french, 17, 31, Sekar B, 11, Stuart G. Porter, cover (bottom), Suede Chen, 9, Wolfgang Zwanzger, cover (top right); Superstock: Jurgen Feuerer/age footstock, 15; Wikimedia/Brain Gratwicke, 21

Artistic elements: Shutterstock: Elena Paletskaya, kavalenkava volha, kotss, La Gorda, mazura1989, Nikiteev_Konstantin, PinkPueblo, Potapov Alexander, Stockobaza, yyang.

We would like to thank Michael Bright for his help in the preparation of this book.

Key

 Mammals

 Birds

 Fish

 Reptiles and amphibians

 Invertebrates

CONTENTS

Some words are shown in bold, **like this**. You can find out what they mean by looking in the glossary.

LET THE GAMES BEGIN!

Every four years, the Olympic Games test the speed, skill and strength of the world's best sportspeople. **Athletics** is the group of track and field events that take place inside the Olympic stadium. It includes running, jumping and throwing competitions.

In any forest, ocean or grassland, you'll find animals that could beat the best human athletes. Speed, jumping and throwing skills are all **adaptations** that help animals to **survive**. Let's find out which animal athletes deserve a medal at the Animalympics!

SPRINT

The 100-metre sprint is one of the oldest Olympic sports. Winners have been recorded since the ancient Olympic Games, which were held more than 2,800 years ago! Today's top **competitors** can run the length of a football pitch in just under 10 seconds. But this is slow compared to the fastest animal athletes.

Spiked shoes help runners grip the track.

🐻 Cheetah

Scientists tracked cheetahs in Botswana and found they could run at up to 93 kilometres (58 miles) per hour. At this speed, they'd cross the finishing line for the 100-metre sprint in less than 6 seconds!

Cheetahs sprint around 170 metres (558 feet) each time they hunt their speedy **prey**. They don't hit their top speed for long.

Peregrine falcon

If the 100-metre sprint were held in the air, the Peregrine falcom would win. No animal can move faster than this bird diving to grab its **prey**. A top speed of almost 390 kilometers (242 miles) per hour lets this bird of prey travel 100 metres (328 feet) in less than a second!

wings tucked close to body

At top speed an Australian tiger beetle like this one can run 170 body lengths per second!

Southern Californian desert mite

For a long time, scientists thought this Australian tiger beetle was the world's fastest animal for its size. Then they discovered a tiny Southern Californian desert mite that zooms along at 322 body lengths per second! The fastest human sprinters only travel six times their body length every second.

9

HIGH JUMP

Human high jumpers must take off from one foot, and soar across the bar without knocking it to the ground. By turning their bodies and arching their backs, top jumpers can clear almost 2.5 metres (8 feet) – the height of a soccer goal.

bar

arched back

foam bed

Salmon

Some fish can out-jump humans. Before salmon **breed**, they swim from the sea back to the river where they hatched. This is often a difficult journey. In some rivers, salmon must leap up waterfalls almost 4 metres (13 feet) high.

churning water gives salmon a boost

🐻 Puma

Big cats are the highest-jumping mammals. Pumas can jump up to a cliff ledge or branch 5.4 metres (nearly 18 feet) above the ground – more than twice as high as the 2.45-metre (8-foot) human record. A cliff ledge or tree is a safe place to sleep or eat, away from hungry food thieves.

Pumas could leap onto the roof of a two-storey house!

 Froghopper

To leap into the air, human high jumpers push against the ground with a **force** two or three times their body weight. A froghopper can push with a force 400 times its body weight, catapulting it 70 centimetres (27.5 inches) into the air. This is like a human leaping 200 metres (656 feet).

MARATHON

The marathon is the longest Olympic running race. Top athletes can complete the 42-km (26-mile) course in 2 hours, but this would just be a warm up for the top animal long-distance runners.

water stop

 # Camel

Camels' bodies are **adapted** for long journeys in the hottest and driest areas of the world. Camels can go for several days without needing to drink. Their ability to cope with heat and thirst means that they can run for more than 18 hours without stopping!

The hump stores fat, which the camel's body breaks down to get energy and water.

long legs

🐻 Pronghorn

Pronghorn, or American antelope, have **adapted** to run fast over long distances. They need to outrun speedy **predators** such as big cats. Pronghorn have been tracked running 11 km (6.8 miles) in just 10 minutes! A cheetah has a higher top speed, but it gets tired much more quickly.

long, thin legs

Even a two-week-old pronghorn can outrun a human!

Ostrich

Ostriches can't fly away from danger. Instead, they run on land. Long legs and springy joints mean ostriches use far less energy than humans as they run. An ostrich could complete a 42-kilometre (26-mile) Olympic marathon in just 50 minutes!

claw digs into the ground for grip

5-metre (16-foot) strides

LONG JUMP

A 30-metre (98.5-foot) run up helps Olympic long jumpers take off at speed. They try to travel as far forward as possible before crash-landing in the sand. Top athletes can jump almost 9 metres (30 feet) – the length of five adult bicycles lined up end to end!

sandpit

🐻 Kangaroo rat

Many animals, such as tigers and kangaroos, can leap further than humans. But the kangaroo rat wins the medal for the mammals. These rodents can jump 20 times their body length, while humans only manage five.

long tail for balance

huge hind feet

Large leaps help kangaroo rats escape **predators** such as snakes.

Jumping spider

Jumping spiders don't spin webs to catch food – they leap on it instead. The two large eyes on the front of the spider's head help it to judge distance. It can make huge leaps up to 40 times its body length.

Six smaller eyes help this jumping spider to spot **prey** moving to its side, and even behind it.

Tree frog

Tree frogs are the champion amphibian jumpers. An average Australian rocket frog jump is 1.2 metres (4 feet) long, but these tiny frogs can leap up to 4 metres (13 feet) – 55 times their body length – to escape from **predators**.

long, powerful legs

rocket-shaped snout

SHOT PUT

Humans are the best throwers in the animal kingdom. Our eyes, shoulders and hands are **adapted** to help us throw all kinds of objects long distances, in the right direction! In Olympic shot put competitions, athletes hold a heavy metal ball and turn quickly to "put" the shot as far as they can.

metal shot

Coconut crab

Coconut crabs can carry a coconut up a tree and throw it back to the ground. The broken coconut is much easier to open and eat. As they are using **gravity** to boost their throws, coconut crabs only get the bronze!

powerful legs

The shot thrown by human athletes weighs 4 kilograms (8.8 pounds) – as much as a typical pumpkin!

Egyptian vulture

When Egyptian vultures spot a tasty ostrich egg, they look for a smooth, rounded stone. They pick up the stone in their beak and throw it at the egg until the thick shell cracks open. Only half of their shots actually hit the eggs!

ostrich egg

Scientists think the vultures once threw the eggs themselves.

 # Chimpanzees

Chimpanzees throw all sorts of things, from stones to poop! They have even been seen collecting objects to throw in the future – showing that just like humans, chimps can plan ahead.

A short thumb means that chimpanzees lose their grip on objects as they swing their arm forwards. Human hands have much longer thumbs, which helps us to grip objects firmly and throw further and faster than any other animal.

AMAZING ADAPTATIONS

Animals don't run, jump and throw objects for sport. The body features that make animals good at running fast, jumping high or throwing well have **adapted** over thousands of years to help them **survive** in certain habitats.

These features help animals to find food, attract mates, look after their young or avoid getting eaten. This means they will get passed on to the next **generation**.

Watching record-breaking animal athletes helps scientists find out how animal bodies work. This information is used in amazing ways, such as designing robots that can move using as little energy as possible.

Springs in this Bionic Kangaroo's legs store energy between jumps, just like the **tendons** of a real kangaroo.

MEDAL TABLE

It's time for the Animalympic medal ceremony! The animal kingdom is divided into groups. Animals with similar features belong to the same class. Which class will take home the most medals for **athletics**?

 ## Mammals

Mammals are warm-blooded animals with hair or fur, that feed milk to their young. They live on the land and in water, and range in size from a bumble-bee-sized bat to the blue whale, the largest animal on earth!

 ## Reptiles and amphibians

Reptiles and amphibians are cold-blooded animals, which means they rely on the Sun's energy to stay warm. Reptiles have dry, scaly skin. Amphibians have moist, smooth skin.

 ## Birds

Birds have feathers, wings and a beak. Most birds can fly, but how will they perform on the running track?

 ## Invertebrates

This group includes all animals without a backbone, such as insects, spiders and snails. Many have a skeleton on the outside of their bodies instead.

 ## Fish

Fish live in salt water or fresh water. They have fins for swimming, and gills to breathe underwater.

RESULTS

EVENT	③ BRONZE	② SILVER	① GOLD
SPRINT	Cheetah	Peregrine falcon	Southern Californian desert mite
HIGH JUMP	Salmon	Puma	Froghopper
MARATHON	Camel	Pronghorn	Ostrich
LONG JUMP	Kangaroo rat	Jumping spider	Tree frog
SHOT PUT	Coconut crab	Egyptian vulture	Chimpanzee

ANIMAL	RANK	GOLD	SILVER	BRONZE
Fish	1	① ①	②	③
Birds	2	①	② ②	③ ③ ③
Mammals	3	①	② ②	
Reptiles and amphibians	4	①		
Invertebrates	5			③

GLOSSARY

adaptation change to the body, workings or behaviour of a living thing that makes it better suited to its habitat

adapted changed to be better suited for an environment

athletics group of sports that include running, jumping and throwing events

breed mate with another animal to produce offspring (babies)

competitor person taking part in a sporting match or contest

force push or pull

generation group of living things that were born, or are living, at about the same time

gravity force that pulls objects down towards the ground

predator animal that hunts and kills other animals for food

prey animal that is hunted and killed by another animal, for food

survive stay alive

tendons the bendy tissue that joins bones to muscles

FIND OUT MORE

Books

Know Your Sport: Track Athletics, Clive Gifford (Franklin Watts, 2012)

Amazing Animal Adaptations series, Julie Murphy (Raintree, 2012)

Websites

Find out about Olympic athletics events at:
http://www.olympic.org/sports

Watch the world's top athletes in action at:
http://www.watchathletics.com/

Find out how to get involved in athletics at any age, at:
http://academy.uka.org.uk/

Find out more about animal adaptations at:
http://www.bbc.co.uk/nature/adaptations

INDEX